GALE
CENGAGE Learning

# Novels for Students, Volume 31

Project Editor: Sara Constantakis Rights Acquisition and Management: Jennifer Altschul, Margaret Chamberlain-Gaston, Leitha Etheridge-Sims, Kelly Quin Composition: Evi Abou-El-Seoud Manufacturing: Drew Kalasky

Imaging: John Watkins

Product Design: Pamela A. E. Galbreath, Jennifer Wahi Content Conversion: Katrina Coach Product Manager: Meggin Condino © 2010 Gale, Cengage Learning

For product information and technology assistance, contact us at **Gale Customer Support, 1-800-877-4253.**

For permission to use material from this text or product, submit all requests online at **www.cengage.com/permissions.**

Further permissions questions can be emailed to **permissionrequest@cengage.com** While every effort has been made to ensure the reliability of the information presented in this publication, Gale, a part of Cengage Learning, does not guarantee the accuracy of the data contained herein. Gale accepts no payment for listing; and inclusion in the publication of any organization, agency, institution, publication, service, or individual does not imply endorsement of the editors or publisher. Errors brought to the attention of the publisher and verified to the satisfaction of the publisher will be corrected in future editions.

*Gale*
27500 Drake Rd.
Farmington Hills, MI, 48331-3535

ISBN-13: 978-1-4144-4169-6
ISBN-10: 1-4144-4169-X
ISSN 1094-3552

This title is also available as an e-book.
ISBN-13: 978-1-4144-4947-0
ISBN-10: 1-4144-4947-X
Contact your Gale, a part of Cengage Learning sales
representative for ordering information.

Printed in the United States of America
1 2 3 4 5 6 7 14 13 12 11 10

# *The Princess Bride*

## William Goldman 1973

## Introduction

*The Princess Bride* is a fantasy romance and adventure novel by William Goldman, first published in 1973 under the full title *The Princess Bride: S. Morgenstern's Classic Tale of True Love and High Adventure, the "Good Parts" Version, Abridged by William Goldman.* Throughout the book, Goldman pretends he is writing an abridgement of a classic work by a writer named S. Morgenstern from the European country of Florin. This is a fictional device; there is no S. Morgenstern, no country called Florin, and no original work called *The Princess Bride* that

Goldman is abridging. The entire work is Goldman's and his alone. He invents the fictional author Morgenstern for a variety of reasons, including humor and satire and the desire to create different ways in which the story may be understood. He frames the main story, about a beautiful girl called Buttercup and her true love, Westley, with another story in which he as an adult looks back on his first encounter with "Morgenstern's" work as a child, when his father read the book to him aloud. As he writes of this childhood encounter with the book, Goldman creates a persona for himself that is equal parts truth and fiction. He presents himself as William Goldman, the author of novels and screenplays (true) who is married to a psychiatrist named Helen with whom he has a ten-year-old son named Jason (fiction). The story itself is an amusing parody of an old-fashioned tale of love and adventure. Goldman tells it with a modern twist, since he refuses to guarantee a happy ending for his two fairy-tale lovers. He also intersperses sections in which he comments about the "original" he is abridging. The result is a comedic satire that also embraces serious themes about love and life.

A thirtieth anniversary edition of *The Princess Bride* was published in 2007 by Houghton Mifflin Harcourt.

# Author Biography

Goldman, a novelist and screenwriter, was born on August 12, 1931, in Chicago, Illinois. In 1952, he graduated from Oberlin College with a B.A. in English and then served in the U.S. Army until 1954. He entered Columbia University and received an M.A. in theater in 1956. Goldman always wanted to become a writer, even though he had not excelled at the creative writing classes he took in college. In 1957, he wrote his first novel, *The Temple of Gold*, which was published by Alfred K. Knopf. After that initial success, Goldman never looked back, although he admitted in an interview with Richard Andersen, published in *William Goldman*, that he did not much enjoy writing and did not consider himself a good writer. He wrote his next novel, *Your Turn to Curtsy, My Turn to Bow* (1958), in seven days, and followed that with several other novels. In 1973, Goldman wrote *The Princess Bride: S. Morgenstern's Classic Tale of True Love and High Adventure, the "Good Parts" Version, Abridged by William Goldman*. He told Andersen that this is the only novel he enjoyed writing and of which he was proud. Goldman used the authorial voice of S. Morgenstern once again when he penned *The Silent Gondoliers*, published in 1983. He has written seventeen novels over the course of his career.

Despite his prolific output as a novelist, Goldman is perhaps best known for his screenplays.

These include *Butch Cassidy and the Sundance Kid* (produced 1969; published 1971); *The Stepford Wives* (1974); *All the President's Men* (1976), based on the book by Bob Woodward and Carl Bernstein (1976); *The Chamber* (1996), written with Chris Reese and adapted from the novel by John Grisham; *Absolute Power* (1997), based on the novel by David Baldacci; and *Dreamcatcher* (2003), written with Lawrence Kasdan and based on the novel by Stephen King.

Goldman also adapted many of his own novels for the screen, including *Marathon Man* (1976), *A Bridge Too Far* (produced in 1977, published as *William Goldman's Story of a Bridge Too Far*, 1977), *Magic* (1978), and *Heat* (1987). Goldman also wrote the screenplay for the movie adaptation of *The Princess Bride* (1987).

During his long career as a writer Goldman has received a number of awards, including the Academy of Motion Picture Arts and Sciences Award (Oscar) for Best Original Screenplay in 1970 for *Butch Cassidy and the Sundance Kid* and a Laurel Award in 1983 for lifetime achievement in screenwriting.

Goldman married Ilene Jones in 1961, and they had two daughters. The marriage ended in divorce. In the early 2000s, he continued to write books of essays and memoirs about his experiences working in Hollywood while continuing his work as a screenwriter.

# Plot Summary

## *Introduction*

    *The Princess Bride* begins with an introduction in which Goldman explains the (fictional) origin of the book. At ten years old, William is lying in bed recuperating from pneumonia, and his immigrant father reads to him from a book called *The Princess Bride*, written by S. Morgenstern, a great author. Like Goldman's father, Morgenstern came from a country called Florin. Young William is too sleepy to take much of it in, but the story sticks in his mind and for the first time in his life he becomes interested in a book. His father reads the entire book to him twice over a month. William then develops a keen interest in adventure stories of all kinds, to the surprise of Miss Roginski, his schoolteacher. Looking back as an adult, Goldman identifies this encounter with *The Princess Bride* to be the best thing that ever happened to him. While in California working on a screenplay, he arranges with a bookstore to deliver a copy of the *The Princess Bride*, in the original Florinese and in an English translation, to his home in New York. He wants Jason, his ten-year-old son, to read it. He returns in two weeks, and when he is having dinner with his wife, Helen, and Jason, the boy says he loved the book, but Goldman soon finds out that Jason read only the first chapter and did not like it. Goldman consults the book himself and finds that it is long and much of it tedious. He realizes that his father only read him the good parts, the sections with all the action. He decides to abridge the book and republish it, the text of which follows.

## *Chapter 1: The Bride*

In Florin, a country between what would later become Sweden and Germany, a beautiful young woman named Buttercup is growing up on the family farm. She is so attractive that all the village boys follow her around, but she is not interested in them. Nor is she interested in the hired hand, whom she simply calls Farm Boy, who lives in a hovel on the farm. She orders him around and he does what he is told.

---

## Media Adaptations

- An abridged version of *The Princess Bride* was released on audio cassette by Dove Audio in 1987. It is read by Rob Reiner, who directed the film version of the book.

- The novel was directed for film by Rob Reiner, with a screenplay written by Goldman. Robin Wright Penn (Buttercup) and Cary Elwes (Westley) starred as the two young lovers. The movie was applauded by critics and audiences for its fidelity to the spirit of the book. It was made by the Twentieth Century-Fox Film Corporation in 1987 and is currently available on DVD and Blu-ray disc.

- *The Princess Bride* was also adapted as a video game, *The Official Princess Bride Game*, by Worldwide Biggies in 2008. It is available for PC, Mac, and Linux computers.

- Though not directly the inspiration, *The Princess Bride* has paved the way for many movies of swashbuckling and romance, including the extremely popular *The Pirates of the Caribbean* movie trilogy, released by Disney from 2003 through 2007, and *Stardust*, a 2007 film produced by Paramount, based on the 1999 Neil Gaiman novel of the same title.

One day, Buttercup's parents, who are always quarreling, see Count and Countess Rugen passing by with an entourage of servants. To the surprise of the farm couple, the procession enters the farm. The Count tells Buttercup's parents that he wants to consult them about their cows, since he has heard they are the best in the land. Buttercup's father is astonished, because he knows their cows are nothing of the kind. In truth, the Count has come just to see the seventeen-year-old Buttercup, since he has heard how beautiful she is. When he sees her, he cannot stop looking at her. Meanwhile, the Countess is quite taken by the appearance of Farm Boy, whose name turns out to be Westley, and she watches him milk the cows as if the secret of how great they are must be in his milking technique. That night, Buttercup reflects on the strange incident. She realizes that the Countess was interested in Westley, and he was interested in her. Then Buttercup realizes that she is jealous. Before dawn she goes to Westley's hovel and declares her eternal love for him. He shuts the door on her without saying a word. Buttercup runs away weeping, but at dusk, Westley comes to her door. She pretends that what she said earlier was a joke, but he cuts her off and says he is leaving for America to make his fortune. He declares his love for Buttercup and wants her to join him when he is rich. Buttercup can hardly believe it, but they soon fall into each other's arms. Over the next few weeks she receives letters from Westley, but then the letters stop. One day her parents tell her that Westley has been killed by pirates off the Carolina coast. Buttercup swears never to love again.

## *Chapter 2: The Groom*

The chapter opens with a section by Goldman explaining that he has cut most of Morgenstern's original chapter because it was mostly about Florinese history. He takes up the story only when it becomes interesting.

Prince Humperdinck, the son of King Lotharon, loves war but loves hunting even more. He likes to kill something every day and has built an underground Zoo of Death, stocked with all kinds of beasts that he can kill. One day he is about to finish off a monkey when Count Rugen brings him the news that his father, King Lotharon, is dying. The Prince is displeased. The death of his father means that he will have to get married so he can produce an heir.

## *Chapter 3: The Courtship*

Humperdinck, Count Rugen, the King, and Queen Bella (Humperdinck's stepmother) agree that Princess Noreena from the neighboring country of Guilder would be a good choice of a bride, and arrangements are made for the Princess to visit. (In one of Goldman's explanatory passages, he notes that he has cut the details of how the visit was arranged because it consisted of over fifty pages detailing the packing and unpacking of clothes and hats). The state dinner for Princess Noreena is a disaster. A fire breaks out, and because the doors are open, there are huge gusts of wind, one of which blows the Princess's hat off, revealing her to be bald. This ensures that the wedding is called off. Prince Humperdinck says he would not mind a commoner as a bride as long as she is beautiful. The Count suggests Buttercup, and the two men go to see her. Humperdinck proposes but she only agrees to marry him when he assures her she will not be required to love him.

## Chapter 4: The Preparations

This chapter consists of a half-page note by Goldman saying that the original chapter by Morgenstern goes on at great length about how Buttercup is made a princess and trained to behave like one, and the King's health improves. This all takes three years, but nothing really happens.

## Chapter 5: The Announcement

Prince Humperdinck introduces the twenty-one-year old Princess Buttercup to a cheering crowd in the great square of Florin City. Later that day, as Buttercup is riding alone, she is kidnapped by three paid assassins: a humpback Sicilian named Vizzini, a Spaniard named Inigo, and a huge Turk named Fezzik. They plan to kill her at the Guilder frontier and make it look like the Guilders are responsible. The purpose is to start a war between Florin and Guilder. The assassins take Buttercup away in a boat; she jumps overboard and swims but is pulled back into the boat before the sharks get her. They reach huge cliffs that they must cross, and they fear they are being followed by another boat. The Sicilian throws a rope that holds fast at the top of the cliff. Fezzik, sinks the boat and carries the other three up the cliff. They are followed by a masked man in black from the boat that followed them. They reach the top and cut the rope, leaving their pursuer hanging from a rock. However, the man keeps climbing. As the others move on, Inigo remains behind to deal with him, and his back story is revealed.

Inigo's father Domingo Montoya was a great sword maker in Spain. One day a nobleman came to him who had six fingers, and he asked Domingo to make him a six-fingered sword. It took Domingo a year of hard work to make the sword. When he returned the nobleman did not like the sword, and when Domingo gave the sword instead to ten-year-old Inigo, the nobleman killed Domingo. Inigo challenged the nobleman, who cut Inigo's face and left. Inigo went to Madrid, Spain, where for two years he was looked after by Yeste, a friend of his father and a famous sword maker. Inigo departed and returned ten years later. He spent the entire time mastering the art of swordsmanship, with the aim of getting revenge on the six-fingered man. He asked Yeste if he was up to the task. Yeste indicated that he was, so Inigo traveled the world for five years in search of his enemy but failed to find him. He started to drink too much and his life went downhill before he was rescued by the Sicilian who recruited him for his criminal activities.

When the man in black reaches the top of the cliff, he and Inigo fight a duel. The advantage swings back and forth but eventually the masked man wins. Because he respects Inigo too much as a swordsman to kill him, the masked man knocks Inigo unconscious and follows the other two assassins. On seeing the man in black coming after them, the Sicilian leaves Fezzik behind to kill him. Fezzik has always been huge, even as a child, but he was also gentle, and his father had to train him to defend himself. He became a fighter and easily defeated all his opponents, even when he was only eleven. When his parents died he joined a traveling circus, but he was too big and too good and the crowds booed him. After he was fired by the circus, Vizzini found him in Greenland and recruited him.

Fezzik and the man in black fight. After a long struggle, the man in black wins, leaves Fezzik exhausted on the ground, and continues the chase. The masked man reaches Vizzini, who is holding a knife at Buttercup's throat. Vizzini boasts about how smart he is, and the man in black challenges him to a battle of wits. The man in black produces some poisonous powder and, out of Vizzini's sight, puts it in one of the two goblets of wine Vizzini has laid out. Vizzini has to choose which glass contains the poison. He guesses wrong, drinks the poisoned goblet and dies. The man in black unties Buttercup and tells her that both glasses were poisoned; he spent years building up his immunity to the poison.

The mysterious man forces the frightened Buttercup to run behind him across the mountainous terrain. They reach a ravine and see below them, in Florin Channel, an armada that Prince Humperdinck has sent to rescue her. Buttercup pushes the man in black down the ravine, from where he removes his mask, revealing himself to be Westley. She tumbles down after him.

At the head of the armada, Prince Humperdinck gazes at the cliff, plotting his next move. He gives instructions to the Count, and the armada splits up, leaving Humperdinck's as the sole ship approaching the coastline. In less than an hour the Prince is on horseback at the top of the cliff, where the Count and a hundred men soon join him. The Prince uses his skill as a hunter to interpret the tracks left by the sword fight and the hand-to-hand fight. He comes upon the dead Vizzini and deduces that two people fell down the ravine. He tells the Count that the ravine opens into the fire swamp.

Westley and Buttercup enter the fire swamp. Westley leads the way, but soon Buttercup disappears in the Snow Sand, a kind of quicksand. Westley dives into it and saves her. He explains to Buttercup how he came to survive: the Dread Pirate Roberts spared his life because Westley made himself so useful. He became Roberts's valet and then second in command. Eventually, Roberts retired and let Westley adopt his name, and Westley is now a feared pirate. His ship is anchored in the bay, and he tells Buttercup that they must reach it. Westley fights off an attack by giant rats, but when they reach the edge of the fire swamp, the Prince and all his forces confront them. Buttercup gets the

Prince to promise he will not hurt Westley, and then she leaves Westley behind. Westley accepts his defeat and is captured. He notices that one of the Count's hands has six fingers.

# *Chapter 6: The Festivities*

Goldman notes that the next section in Morgenstern is boring, since it deals at length with all the festivities leading up to the wedding of Buttercup and the Prince that is to take place in three months. Goldman skips forward a month and returns to the story of Inigo, who regains consciousness and makes his way to the Thieves Quarter in Florin City, hoping to meet up with Vizzini. Meanwhile Fezzik finds Vizzini dead and goes searching for Inigo. He ends up at a village being taunted by the local boys.

Westley awakes in an underground cage in the Zoo of Death, guessing that he will be tortured. Meanwhile, the King dies and the Prince ascends to the throne. He is very busy learning how to conduct affairs of state so the wedding to Buttercup is not as big as planned. As the couple stands on the balcony, an old woman boos the new queen for choosing gold over love. Then Buttercup awakes from a nightmare; she is not in fact married yet. She has a series of nightmares, all related to her choice to walk away from Westley in the fire swamp. She tells the Prince she made a mistake and she really loves Westley. The Prince appears to be sympathetic and says he will allow her to marry

Westley if he still wants to marry her. In truth, it is the Prince who hired the assassins and he now plans to kill Buttercup on their wedding night, blame it on the Guilders, and start a war.

Count Rugen tortures Westley while the Prince questions him, trying to get him to say who hired him to kidnap Buttercup. Westley truthfully denies that anyone hired him. He resists the pain by thinking of Buttercup. The Prince helps Buttercup write to Westley, and she lets slip the information that Westley is frightened of Spinning Ticks. That night Westley is tortured by having Spinning Ticks placed on his skin. Next, the Count tortures him with a fiendish device called the Machine.

Meanwhile, the Prince orders the Thieves Quarter to be cleared out by his thugs, the Brute Squad, since he fears the Guilders are there, plotting a covert attack on his kingdom. One of the Brutes turns out to be Fezzik, who was hired for his strength. Fezzik finds Inigo, and together they take refuge in an alehouse in the now empty quarter. Inigo wants to kill the Count to avenge his father, but he needs the help of the man in black, so Inigo and Fezzik seek him out. Meanwhile Buttercup has found out that the Prince never sent her letter to Westley asking if he still wished to marry her. She calls him a coward. Outraged, the Prince goes to the Zoo of Death and murders Westley.

## Chapter 7: The Wedding

Fezzik and Inigo enter the Zoo of Death. They

go past caged animals down to the third level, where they beat off an attack by snakes. At level four, Fezzik is terrified by bats, but Inigo kills them with his sword. At the fifth level they find Westley's body, which they take to Miracle Max, a healer who used to be employed by the king. They tell Max they need a miracle. After much argument and negotiation, which also involves Max's wife Valerie, Max agrees to bring Westley back to life. Inigo and Fezzik gather ingredients for a resurrection pill that will work for only one hour.

It is the day of the wedding, and the Prince is still plotting to murder Buttercup that night and frame the Guilderians for the crime. Fifty minutes before the wedding, Inigo and Fezzik feed Westley the pill and he revives. The wedding ceremony has begun as the three men advance on the castle guard. Fezzik terrifies the guards by claiming to be the Dread Pirate Roberts and appearing to burst into flames, although only his coat is on fire.

## Chapter 8: The Honeymoon

Fezzik, Inigo, and Westley enter the castle, although unknown to them they are too late to stop the wedding. Inigo confronts the Count, who runs away. Buttercup goes to the Prince's chamber, intent on suicide. Fezzik, Inigo, and Westley get separated, and Inigo pursues the Count. When Inigo catches him, the Count stabs him with a dagger. However, Inigo fights on, and eventually the Count dies of fright when he realizes that Inigo will cut his heart out. Meanwhile, Westley has made it to Buttercup, but they are found by the Prince. Westley threatens to mutilate him, which frightens the Prince. Buttercup then ties up Humperdinck. Inigo and Fezzik arrive, and the four make their escape on horseback to the Florin Channel.

Goldman comments that when his father read him the story, he ended it there, but Morgenstern made the ending more ambiguous. The four are pursued by the Prince, and each meets with a setback. The final outcome of their escape is unstated.

## *Queen Bella*

Queen Bella is King Lotharon's wife and Prince Humperdinck's stepmother. He calls her the evil stepmother, but actually she is sweet and considerate and much beloved in the kingdom.

## *Buttercup*

Buttercup grows up on a farm and at the age of fifteen is potentially one of the most beautiful women in the world. However, she does not care about beauty or about the hired hand she calls Farm Boy who works on her family's farm. When she is nearly seventeen she falls in love with the Farm Boy, Westley, and starts to take some trouble with her appearance. Within a few weeks she goes from being the twentieth most beautiful woman in the world to ninth, and is still rising. She is happy to wait while Westley makes his fortune in America and is devastated when she hears about Westley's death at the hands of pirates. She vows never to love again. When Prince Humperdinck, seeking a beautiful bride, asks her to marry him, she agrees only on the condition that she will not be required to love him. When Westley rescues her from kidnappers, she once more expresses her love for him. When they are cornered by Prince Humperdinck she surrenders to the Prince rather than dying with Westley, admitting that she can live without love. She later has nightmares in which she regrets her choice, and she remains calm as her wedding to Prince Humperdinck takes place, knowing that Westley will come to save her.

## *Buttercup's Father*

Buttercup's father is a farmer who is not good at anything. He is neither a good farmer nor a good husband. He and his wife spend much of their time squabbling, each trying to score points in a running argument.

## *Buttercup's Mother*

Buttercup'smother worries a lot and is a bad cook. She always wanted to be popular, but it never happened. What keeps her alive is her endless fighting with her husband. When he dies, she dies soon after, as if she could not live without him.

## *Falkbridge*

Falkbridge owns an alehouse in the Thieves Quarter. He practically runs the Thieves Quarter and has a hand in almost every crime that goes on there. To escape jail he regularly pays a bribe to Yellin.

## *Farm Boy*

*See* Westley

# Fezzik

Fezzik is a huge, gentle Turk who is recruited by Vizzini to help kidnap Buttercup. When Fezzik was one year old, he already weighed eighty-five pounds, and he started shaving when he was in kindergarten. Fezzik is incredibly strong. He once held up an elephant using only the muscles in his back, and his arms are tireless. However, he is not very bright and always has to be told what to do. Even so, he is fascinated by words and loves to make rhymes. When Fezzik is put to the test in the fight with Westley, he comes up short; Westley is the first person to beat him. However, Fezzik proves his worth later on, terrifying the guards outside the castle and allowing Buttercup's rescuers to enter.

# Billy Goldman

*See* William Goldman

# Helen Goldman

Helen Goldman is the author's fictional wife. She has a brilliant intellect and is a child psychiatrist. However, she does not seem to be very skillful in handling people, and her marriage to William seems unhappy. He thinks she lacks a sense of humor.

# Jason Goldman

Jason Goldman is the ten-year-old son of

William and Helen Goldman. He is an overweight boy who eats too much, and his father thinks that, like his mother, Jason lacks a sense of humor. His father gives him an unabridged copy of *The Princess Bride* to read but Jason finds it boring. This gives William the idea to abridge the book to include only the interesting parts.

## William Goldman

William Goldman is the author of the novel in which he also appears as a character. The character is a careful mixture of fact and fiction. In the novel, Goldman is, as in real life, the successful author of screenplays such as *Butch Cassidy and the Sundance Kid* and *The Stepford Wives*, and the novel *The Temple of Gold*, which was published when he was twenty-six. However, most of the rest is a fictional creation. Goldman the fictional character is married to a child psychiatrist and has an overweight son. He also remembers hearing his father read *The Princess Bride* to him when he was ten, an experience that was instrumental in giving him a love of literature that no doubt contributed to his career as a writer. His wife thinks he is emotionally needy, and he admits that he does not love her. In spite of this, when he is away they talk to each other every day on the phone.

## William Goldman's Father

The fictional William Goldman's father was a nearly illiterate immigrant from Florin who worked as a barber in Highland Park, Illinois. With great difficulty, and in a tongue that was foreign to him, he reads *The Princess Bride* to his ten-year-old son, but he skips through the boring parts. He also shows a sensitivity to his son's feelings. He wants to skip the part where Wesley dies and he omits the ambiguous ending so that Billy (as he called his son) would think the story ended happily.

## Hiram Haydn

Hiram Haydn is Goldman's editor at Harcourt Brace Jovanovich. Goldman calls him in the middle of the night to suggest an abridgement of Morgenstern's classic story.

## Prince Humperdinck

Prince Humperdinck is the son of King Lotharon and the heir to the throne. He is a huge, barrel-chested man who weighs about 250 pounds. He likes war but loves hunting so much he builds an underground Zoo of Death that contains all varieties of creatures, so he can amuse himself by hunting and killing them. He has no friends and confides only in Count Rugen. It soon becomes apparent that Humperdinck is a villain of the highest order. After he gets Buttercup to marry him he hires some assassins to kidnap her and dump her on the frontier of Guilder, the neighboring country, so he can blame Guilder for her death and start a war. He has wanted to conquer Guilder since he was a boy. When his first plan is foiled by Westley's rescue of

Buttercup he devises another one, in which he will personally kill Buttercup on her wedding night and blame her death on soldiers from Guilder. Humperdinck's true nature is fully revealed when Buttercup calls him a coward. Outraged, he throws her into her room and locks the door, then goes to the Zoo of Death where he murders Westley.

## King Lotharon

King Lotharon is the king of Florin. He is very old and sick and can speak only by muttering and mumbling.

## The Man in Black

*See* Westley

## Miracle Max

Miracle Max is a healer who tended the king but was fired by Prince Humperdinck. This caused him to lose all his patients, and he now lives in a hut with his wife, Valerie. When Inigo and Fezzik bring the dead Westley to him, saying they need a miracle, Max at first refuses, saying he is retired. He agrees to bring Westley back from the dead only when he learns that Westley will stop Humperdinck's marriage.

## Domingo Montoya

Domingo Montoya was Inigo's father. He was

a master sword maker from the village of Arabella in the mountains of northern Spain who met his death when a nobleman for whom he had made a six-fingered sword was dissatisfied with the product and, after an argument, killed him. His son Inigo has sworn to avenge his father's death.

## *Inigo Montoya*

Inigo Montoya is a Spaniard who is a master swordsman. He developed his skills over many years of study and travel because he wanted to avenge his father's death at the hands of a six-fingered nobleman. He witnessed this event when he was ten years old. After traveling the world for five years but failing to find his enemy, Inigo starts to drink and lose his purpose in life. He is rescued by Vizzini and recovers his sword fighting skills as a member of Vizzini's criminal gang. He is bested by Westley in a sword fight but teams up with him to confront and kill Count Rugen, the six-fingered man, in the castle.

## *Edith Neisser*

Edith Neisser wrote books about the psychology of human relationships. The fictional Goldman writes that he knew Neisser (a real person) when he was in his teens because they lived in the same town. It was Neisser who first told him that life is not fair.

## Dread Pirate Roberts

*See* Westley

## Miss Roginksi

Miss Roginksi is Goldman's teacher from third to fifth grade at Highland Park Grammar School. She calls him a late bloomer because he is not good at academic subjects. When he later sends her a copy of his first novel, he is relieved to find that she remembers him.

## Count Rugen

Count Rugen is a big man with black hair and six fingers on his right hand. He is the only Count in Florin and is a confidant of Prince Humperdinck. The Count is an accomplished man and Humperdinck depends on him for his skills as an architect and inventor. The Count designed crucial elements of the Zoo of Death and invented the torture device known as the Machine. He is interested in pain and is writing a book about it. Many years ago he murdered Domingo Montoya, and he eventually gets his comeuppance when Inigo tracks him down. They engage in a sword fight, but the Count dies of fright when he realizes that Inigo is about to cut his heart out.

## Countess Rugen

The Countess is the wife of the Count and is

much admired, and also feared, in Florin. She is much younger than her husband and is considered to embody the height of taste and fashion. She acquires her clothes from Paris and eventually settles there.

## Sandy Sterling

Sandy Sterling is a Hollywood starlet. Goldman meets her at the hotel swimming pool when he is in California. She tells him that *The Stepford Wives* is one of her favorite books and that she would do anything to be in the movie.

## Six-fingered Man

*See* Count Rugen

## Valerie

Valerie is Miracle Max's wife. She encourages him to come to an agreement with Inigo and resurrect Westley because she and Max need the money.

## Vizzini

The hunchback Vizzini is a Sicilian criminal who is hired by Humperdinck to kidnap and kill Buttercup. Vizzini recruits Inigo and Fezzik to help him do the job. Vizzini is the undisputed leader of the group and he prides himself on his intelligence and cunning. He tells Westley that he is "the slickest, sleekest, sliest and wiliest fellow who has yet come down the pike." But this formidable assembly of qualities does not enable him to outwit Westley, who tricks him into drinking a poisoned goblet of wine.

## *Westley*

Westley is an orphan who was taken on by Buttercup's father to work on the farm. He lives in a hovel but keeps it clean and reads by candlelight. Buttercup, however, thinks he is stupid and treats him with contempt as her virtual slave. She calls him Farm Boy. Westley is in fact handsome, muscular, and intelligent, and he has already fallen in love with Buttercup. After Buttercup finally realizes that she is in love with him too, he goes to America to make his fortune so that she can come and join him later. Within a few months, Westley is reputed to have been killed by pirates; but this is not so: he has become the Dread Pirate Roberts. He returns to Florin to save Buttercup from her abductors and then rescue her from Prince Humperdinck. Westley is the ideal hero throughout the story. He is a better fighter than either Inigo or Fezzik, and he cannot be forced by torture into lying. He never stops loving Buttercup and is brought back from the dead solely because his love is true. Also, he lives for longer than the resurrection pill should allow because he asks the "Lord of Permanent Affection" for the strength to stay alive for the entire day.

## Yellin

Yellin is the head of law enforcement in Florin City. He is a crafty man who takes bribes.

## Yeste

Yeste was a rich, fat master sword maker from Madrid who was a friend of Domingo Montoya. After Domingo was killed, Yeste looked after his son Inigo for two years.

## *The Unfairness of Life*

The reader might expect this fantasy romantic/adventure novel to follow the usual pattern of such stories: good is always rewarded, evil perishes, and the good characters live happily ever after. But this is not entirely the case in *The Princess Bride*. The author is at pains to show that life is not fair, that it can be disappointing and not measure up to one's hopes and dreams. In this sense he introduces a strong note of realism into the tale. The theme that life is not fair occurs both in the passages Goldman inserts where he comments on his own life and the "original" Morgenstern story, as well as in the tale itself. In the introduction, in which Goldman describes how he came to write the book, he explains that he once thought his life would follow the subtitle of the story and be all about "true love and high adventure," but it did not happen. In particular, his fictional self admits that he is not especially happy in his marriage, and he adds, "I don't know if I love anything truly any more beyond the porterhouse at Peter Luger's and the cheese enchilada at El Parador's." It is a light-hearted comment with serious undertones, and it is relevant for the story that follows, since it serves as ironic, real-life commentary (although of course the real-life element is also a fiction) on the romance and future prospects of Buttercup and Westley. The theme of the unfairness of life is stated explicitly in the section in which Goldman comments on his own reaction when as a boy his father read to him the part about Buttercup marrying Humperdinck. Even a ten-year-old knows that in stories like *The Princess Bride* such things do not happen. Yet they do. This leaves the young boy with the disappointed feeling that something is not right, both in the story and in life, and this feeling remains with him even as an adult. He recalls that when he was in his teens, an acquaintance of his named Edith Neisser (who was a real-life author of books on psychology) explained to him:

> Life isn't fair, Bill. We tell our children that it is, but it's a terrible thing to do. It's not only a lie, it's a cruel lie. Life is not fair, and it never has been, and it's never going to be.

The theme of the unfairness of life continues when the young William Goldman's father does not want to read him the chapter in which Westley dies. Young William is horrified when he learns that the hero dies, and also that no one kills the evil Prince Humperdinck. This little episode enacts exactly what Edith later explained. The story being read reflects the unfairness of life, but the parent is very reluctant for the child to discover this distressing fact.

## *True Love versus Love of Power*

Although the author keeps reminding the

reader that life is unfair, this does not stop him from writing a story which shows the enduring power of love and its capacity to defeat evil. Buttercup and Westley genuinely love each other and prove it again and again. Westley overcomes everything in his path to claim Buttercup as his bride. Buttercup never for a moment betrays Westley by loving Prince Humperdinck; she surrenders to the Prince only when she has made him promise that he will not hurt Westley. She cannot bear that Westley should suffer.

The story also shows that love has the capacity to enhance and prolong life. When, for example, Westley asks the "Lord of Permanent Affection" to extend the efficacy of the resurrection pill for the rest of the day, his wish is granted. In contrast, the torture machine has the effect of subtracting life. The machine sucks ten years from Westley's life in just a week. This neatly shows what Prince Humperdinck and the Count represent: they are the anti-life forces; they exist only to dominate others, to revel in their own power and cruelty. Humperdinck is the classic evil character. He has no tender feelings for Buttercup; he only loves war and hunting. Buttercup is just another form of prey for him, since he plots to kill her so he can create a pretext that will allow him to indulge his other love —he wants to make war with Guilder. As for the Count, his only interest is in pain, and he has the coldheartedness to inflict it on others without a qualm. When he is finally killed by Inigo and is forced to suffer the same fear that he liked to inflict, this is also an illustration of the power of love: the love of a son for his murdered father.

---

# Topics for Further Study

- Read *Stardust* (1999), a fairy tale about a prince and his adventures on behalf of his beloved, by Neil Gaiman. In a written report, compare this book to *The Princess Bride*. What do the two books have in common in terms of theme and style, and how do they differ? Wherein lies their appeal? As an alternative to *Stardust*, you may choose *The Neverending Story* (1983) by Michael Ende.

- Watch the movie version of *The Princess Bride*. Working with another student, analyze how the film compares to the book. What elements are changed? In what sense is it true to the original? Are the actors well cast in their roles? Give a class presentation in which you discuss your findings, using PowerPoint and images to support your argument. Also include clips from the film if possible.

- Write a short romantic fable, fantasy, or fairy tale in which you mix the traditional and the modern to create an amusing effect. Read folktales and fairy tales from other cultures to support your new story. Does your story express fairy-tale ideals, remote from the way real life happens, or does it also, like *The Princess Bride*, have a serious message? Using your design skills, add some pictures that contribute to the story's appeal and create an appealing page layout.

- Research the current divorce rate in the United States. Is it going up or down? Why do so many marriages fail? Is there any connection between a high divorce rate and our society's acceptance of romantic love as the main basis for marriage? How would you describe romantic love? With another student, lead a class discussion on this topic, using *The Princess Bride* as a way of

The struggle between the power of love and the love of power is illustrated in one of the most dramatic moments in the novel, the long scream that Westley utters as he dies, which is heard all over Florin City. Inigo recognizes it as "the sound of Ultimate Suffering." The scream expresses the terrible pain that occurs when a genuine and deep love is sundered by the cruel murder of one of the lovers. It represents the apparent triumph of evil over good, the anguish of life when love is extinguished. But, significantly, this scream is not the last sound in the novel, and nor is it without positive effect. It inspires Inigo to find Westley quickly, and when he and Fezzik take the dead man to Miracle Max, it is because Westley, thanks to Max's ingenious use of the bellows, says that he wants to live because of true love that Max (with a little prodding from his wife) agrees to bring him back. There is something about love that will not be defeated despite all the forces arrayed against it.

## *Parody*

The novel is part fairy tale, part fantasy, part adventure, and part romance, but it is all these things only with a twist. The author is familiar with these genres and is determined to parody them. A parody is a spoof in which something—a style, a genre—is imitated only to make fun of it.

The fairy-tale element includes the beautiful girl who becomes a princess and marries a prince. Fantasy literature often includes events, creatures, and situations that could not happen in real life, such as the climbing of the Cliffs of Insanity, fighting giant snakes and rodents, and making the resurrection pill. The adventure story is all action, including the kind of fights and chases that take place in *The Princess Bride*. The presentation of Inigo as the greatest swordsman in the world is a nod to *The Three Musketeers* (1844), the adventure novel by Alexandre Dumas that the fictional Goldman mentions reading as a boy in the introduction. The romantic element in the novel is obvious: the love of Westley and Buttercup is the central fabric around which the story is woven.

However, the elements of parody are not difficult to spot. In the first chapter the fairy-tale cliché of the most beautiful woman of the world is parodied in the figure of Buttercup, who has potential but has to work her way up into the top ten rankings. Inspired by her love for Westley, she races up the charts, moving from twentieth, to fifteenth and then up to ninth, and is still on the rise. The humor works by anachronism (being chronologically out of place): the modern concept of the Top Ten ranking list for this or that is juxtaposed with a fable set mostly in medieval times, and this makes it stand out as funny.

The fairy-tale element, as well as the conventions of the popular romance, are parodied in the exaggerated language with which Buttercup and Westley first declare their love for each other. They go completely overboard, as this quotation, spoken by Buttercup, shows:

> I have loved you for several hours now, and every second, more. I thought an hour ago that I loved you more than any woman has ever loved a man, but a half hour after that I knew that what I felt before was nothing compared to what I felt then.

And so on.

The description of Westley as handsome, tanned, and muscular is a parody of the bare-chested hero who appears on the covers of countless romance novels that adorn the supermarket racks. However, there is an extra joke there too, because at the time Buttercup is so naive she does not yet perceive Westley as the attractive man he obviously is. Puzzled by the Countess's interest in him, she concludes that the noble lady must be attracted to him because he has good teeth, although this explanation does not end her puzzlement.

Another parody is that the prince whom the princess marries is not her true love (as in a fairy tale) but rather the evil Prince Humperdinck. The parody shows up in the title of the second chapter. Having introduced the bride in chapter 1, and the apparent groom, Westley, the author then kills off Westley (or so it seems) and devotes chapter 2, "The Groom," to Prince Humperdinck. Clearly, this is no ordinary romance, and certainly in no traditional romance would the hero die by torture at the hands of his enemy. Just in case the reader should miss these obvious parodies, Goldman draws attention to them through the device of his ten-year-old fictional self, who is hearing the story read by his father.

## Symbolism

Recurring symbolism of rebirth enhances the theme of the power of love and the capacity of life to renew itself in the name of good. The first examples are Inigo and Fezzik. They are both "good" characters but when they are first introduced they are rather less than that. Allowing their own failures and disappointments in life to obscure their true natures, they have been recruited by Vizzini for his criminal gang. However, both undergo a kind of rebirth when they are defeated and knocked unconscious by the man in black (Westley). This breaks their attachment to criminality, and when they recover they eventually find their way back to more positive endeavors. Instead of being part of a three-member criminal enterprise, they form another gang of three, with Westley replacing Vizzini, dedicated to ensuring the triumph of love and goodness.

Westley is also the agent of another symbolic rebirth when Buttercup falls into the snow sand in the fire swamp. She goes through a near death experience: "She was just falling, gently, through this soft, powdery mass, falling farther and farther from anything resembling life." She would have died had it not been for Westley coming to the rescue. The incident shows that there is nothing that Westley cannot or will not do for her. He is like Orpheus, the hero in the ancient Greek myth who goes down to Hades (the underworld) to recover his bride Euridice.

Westley undergoes the most dramatic rebirth of them all, but even before Miracle Max's resurrection pill is forced down his throat, he has already been symbolically reborn twice. After all, Buttercup is informed that Westley has been killed by pirates, and the reader knows no better until the man in black reveals in the ravine that he is Westley. Later, Westley explains that he eventually took on the identity of the Dread Pirate Roberts, which is another symbolic rebirth. This shows that he was able to do what he had to do in order to survive. Finally, Westley's literal resurrection from the dead shows the power of love to triumph even over death itself.

# The Fantasy Novel

Goldman published *The Princess Bride* at a time when the fantasy novel was gaining popularity. Much of the new interest in fantasy was fueled by the success of J. R. R. Tolkien's *The Hobbit* (1937) and the *Lord of the Rings* trilogy (1954-55), which became extremely popular in the United States in the late 1960s. C. S. Lewis's seven-volume *Chronicles of Narnia* (1950-56), written for children but also read by adults, also contributed to the growing interest in fantasy literature. The first great fantasy work to be published in the United States following the wave of interest in Tolkien was Ursula K. Le Guin's *Earthsea Trilogy* (1968-72), written for young adults but read by a far wider group for its psychological insight. The trilogy is set in the fantasy islands of Earthsea and shows the coming of age of a young wizard. Another of the most popular fantasy writers of the period was Terry Brooks, whose first book, *The Sword of Shannara* (1977) reached the *New York Times* bestseller list. Brooks followed this with many other books during the 1980s and 1990s, making him one of the most successful fantasy writers of all time. He had, and still has, a large following among young-adult readers.

With the growth of fantasy literature, a

scholarly interest in defining and categorizing it also began to grow. For Ann Swinfen, in *In Defense of Fantasy: A Study of the Genre in English and American Literature since 1945*, "The essential ingredient of all fantasy is 'the marvellous' ... anything outside the normal space-time continuum of the everyday world." Brian Attebery, in *The Fantasy Tradition in American Literature: From Irving to Le Guin*, offered another broad definition of fantasy: a story that "treat[s] an impossibility as if it were true." He suggested that fantasy can then be further defined into subcategories based on elements such as "the marvelous within the story, the orientation of the tale toward wonder or its obverse, horror, the location of the supernatural in another world or in this," and other elements.

Among the subcategories of fantasy, many of which overlap, are high fantasy, such as Tolkien, in which there is a titanic moral struggle between good and evil; animal fantasy, which features talking animals, as in Richard Adams's *Watership Down*, published in 1972; heroic fantasy, sometimes also called "sword and sorcery," which focuses on action and adventure; historical fantasy; time travel fantasy; romantic fantasy; and others.

## Compare & Contrast

- **Medieval Era:** This is the age of chivalric romance, in which many popular stories feature brave knights who fight for justice in battles between good and evil. People believe in great heroes and their exploits.

**1970s:** At the height of the difficult and unpopular Vietnam War, and with the Watergate scandal in Washington politics, there are few heroes to be found. War is no longer perceived as glamorous and exciting but as a last resort in settling disputes between nations.

**Today:** Heroes are less often found in military or political figures, but instead are often ordinary people who show great bravery in unexpected, dangerous situations. An example is Wesley Autrey, a construction worker in Harlem, New York, who is a Vietnam War veteran. Autrey jumps down onto the subway tracks to save a man who has had a seizure and fallen on the tracks. Autrey lies on top of the man in the ditch between the rails as the train passes over both of them. Then-President George W. Bush later acknowledges Autrey's bravery during his State of the Union address.

- **Medieval Era:** This era produces two of the great love stories of all time. Gottfried von Strassburg writes his poem "Tristan and Iseult" (first transcribed in 1210), and the real-life Abelard and Heloise live out a romance in the twelfth century that, through their letters to each other, becomes famous through the ages. Abelard is a philosopher and theologian, and Heloise is also an accomplished scholar.

**1970s:** Love stories still have the power to entrance and delight. Eric Segal's *Love Story* (1970), which tells the story of a tragic love, becomes a bestseller and is made into the equally popular movie of the same name starring Ryan O'Neal and Ali MacGraw.

**Today:** In the age of short attention spans and 140-character messages on the social networking and micro-blogging service Twitter, love stories are much shorter. Harper Perennial publishes *Six-Word Memoirs on Love & Heartbreak: By Writers Famous and Obscure* (2009), in which people sum up their experience of love in just six words.

- **Medieval Era:** In war and battle, combat is often hand-to-hand; there are few weapons that can kill at a distance.

**1970s:** Nuclear weapons are capable of traveling across continents, and a nuclear war could annihilate human civilization in a matter of hours.

**Today:** One of the chief threats to world peace is nuclear weapons in the hands of terrorists or so-called rogue states.

---

*The Princess Bride* is hard to place in any one fantasy category. With its vaguely medieval setting and battle between good and evil, it resembles high fantasy, and there are also elements in the story of heroic and romantic fantasy. But often these kinds of fantasies are serious works, in the sense that they do not contain much humor. In contrast, Goldman's book bubbles over with humorous characters, dialogue, and scenes. This aligns him most closely with other fantasies from the same period that employ liberal doses of humor. One example is *Bored of the Rings* (1969), by Henry N. Beard and Douglas C. Kenney, a comic parody of Tolkien's *Lord of the Rings*. The popular "Xanth" books by Piers Anthony, beginning with *A Spell for Chameleon* (1977), provide more examples of comic fantasy, as do British author Terry Pratchett's "Discworld" series, beginning with *The Color of Magic* in 1983.

# Critical Overview

*The Princess Bride* garnered several positive reviews when it was first published in 1973. In *Newsweek*, S. K. Oberbeck recommends it as a "charming hoax" and a "ridiculously swashbuckling fable" that "sounds like all the Saturday serials you ever saw feverishly reworked by the Marx brothers." In the *New York Times Book Review*, Gerald Walker shows a similar appreciation, commenting on the "witty, affectionate send-up of the adventure-yarn form." Walker also notes the effect of the passages in which Goldman interrupts the narrative to explain what he is doing, commenting that this introduces "a kind of comedic extension of Brecht's distancing effect, alienation to provoke not an intellectual response, but an *entertained* response. And it works." Walker is referring to the German dramatist Bertolt Brecht (1898-1956), whose "distancing effect" was aimed at preventing an audience from identifying too strongly with the characters and encouraging them to remain aware that they were watching a play, an artificial construct designed so that the audience would be better able to reflect on and evaluate the play. The novel is also positively evaluated by Liz Holliday in *St. James Guide to Fantasy Writers*. She admires Goldman's storytelling skills and calls the novel an "immensely enjoyable romp." She further comments, "As with all the best fairy tales, the characters are cardboard cutouts—but Goldman pulls off a real trick by making us care for them all."

# What Do I Read Next?

- *The Silent Gondoliers* (1983) is another work by the great S. Morgenstern (a pseudonym for Goldman) about why the famous gondoliers of Venice no longer sing. Told with Goldman's typical humor, it is the story of Luigi, an aspiring gondolier.

- In 1998, a twenty-fifth anniversary edition of *The Princess Bride* was published. It includes not only a new introduction by Goldman, in which he discusses the film version, it also includes a the first chapter of a sequel to *The Princess Bride* titled "Buttercup's Baby," and an introductory "explanation" by

Goldman as to how this new "abridgement" of "Morgenstern" came about.

- *Like Water for Chocolate* (1995) is a first novel by Mexican writer Laura Esquivel. Set in Mexico about a hundred years ago, it tells the story of life in a Mexican family. The main character is Tita, the youngest daughter, who falls in love with Pedro but is not allowed to marry him because she must take care of her aging mother. The novel was a bestseller in Mexico and the United States.

- British fantasy author Diana Wynne Jones writes for young-adult readers. She is noted for her excellent plotting and well-realized fantasy worlds. *Howl's Moving Castle* (1986) was one of five Jones novels to be named by the American Library Association as one of the Best Books for Young Adults. The story focuses on Sophie, a teenage girl who must lift the curse that has turned her into an old woman. Jones tells the tale with plenty of humor.

- *The Three Musketeers* is a famous adventure story by Alexandre Dumas, first published in France in 1844 and available in translation in many modern editions. Set in seventeenth-century France, it features the adventures of three of the king's musketeers, Athos, Porthos, and Aramis, and their friend, d'Artagnan, as they defend the interests of the king and queen against the schemes of Cardinal Richelieu.

- *On a Pale Horse* (1983), by prolific fantasy writer Piers Anthony, appeared on the American Library Association list of Best Books for Young Adults in 1984. The book is the first in Anthony's popular series "Incarnations of Immortality," in which abstract concepts such as death, fate, and time are personified. In this book, the hero, Zane, and other powerful figures, such as a magician, must stop Satan from starting World War III.

- Some readers may prefer their romantic tales without the ironies and parodies that Goldman embeds in *The Princess Bride*. For such readers Nicholas Sparks's bestseller, *A Walk to Remember* (1999), might make a good choice. This story about two young people in North Carolina in the 1950s is as romantic as it gets, and Sparks's unadorned style and storytelling skills make it hard to put down. Oddly enough, like *The Princess Bride*, it also has a rather ambiguous ending, and readers are free to interpret it in an optimistic or a pessimistic light.

# Sources

Andersen, Richard, *William Goldman*, Twayne's United States Author Series, No. 326, Twayne Publishers, 1979, pp. 16, 82.

Attebery, Brian, *The Fantasy Tradition in American Literature: From Irving to Le Guin*, Indiana University Press, 1980, pp. 2-3.

Buckley, Cara, "Man Is Rescued by Stranger on Subway Tracks," in *New York Times*, January 3, 2007, http://www.nytimes.com/2007/01/03/nyregion/03life_r=2&ref=nyregion&oref=slogin (accessed April 20, 2009).

Goldman, William, *The Princess Bride: S. Morgenstern's Classic Tale of True Love and High Adventure, The "Good Parts" Version, Abridged by William Goldman*, Harcourt Brace, 1973.

Holliday, Liz, "The Princess Bride," in *St. James Guide to Fantasy Writers*, edited by David Pringle, St. James Press, 1996, p. 235.

MacRae, Cathi Dunn, *Presenting Young Adult Fantasy Fiction*, Twayne's United States Authors Series, No. 699, Twayne Publishers, 1998.

Oberbeck, S. K., "Shaggy Dog," in *Newsweek*, Vol. 82, No. 12, September 17, 1973, p. 98.

Swinfen, Ann, *In Defense of Fantasy: A Study of the Genre in English and American Literature since*

*1945*, Routledge & Kegan Paul, 1984, p. 5.

Walker, Gerald, "The Princess Bride," in the *New York Times Book Review*, December 23, 1973, p. 14.

# Further Reading

Armitt, Lucie, *Fantasy Fiction: An Introduction*, Continuum, 2005.

> This is an introduction to a wide range of fantasy fiction, including the work of Jonathan Swift, J. R. R. Tolkien, George Orwell, H. G. Wells, J. K. Rowling, and many others. The book includes a useful introduction defining the genre and a chapter on the origins of modern fantasy, as well as a glossary of terms.

Brady, John, *The Craft of the Screenwriter*, Touchstone, 1982.

> Brady includes interviews with many of the most successful screenwriters of the 1970s, including Goldman, Robert Towne, and Paul Schrader.

Goldman, William, *Adventures in the Screen Trade: A Personal View of Hollywood and Screenwriting*, Warner, 1983.

> This book will be useful for those who have enjoyed the films for which Goldman wrote the screenplays. He reflects on his twenty-year involvement with Hollywood, gives his views on the

film industry, and provides individual chapters on some of his most well-known films, including *Butch Cassidy and the Sundance Kid*, *The Stepford Wives*, and *All the President's Men*.

Le Guin, Ursula K., *The Language of the Night: Essays on Fantasy and Science Fiction*, rev. ed., Perennial, 1993.

Goldman once commented that he felt very close to his subconscious mind during the writing of *The Princess Bride*, but he said nothing further about it. In the essays that make up this book, one of the greatest writers of fantasy explores, among many other things, the creative process and how it taps into dreams and archetypes.